MW00895355

Go!

From Studio Audience
to Center Stage

Arron Chambers
+ Nancy Karpenske

Standard®
PUBLISHING
Bringing The Word to Life

Cincinnati, Ohio

Published by Standard Publishing, Cincinnati, Ohio, www.standardpub.com.
Copyright © 2009 Standard Publishing

Go!, ISBN 978-0-7847-2282-4, © 2009 Standard Publishing

Project editor: Lynn Lusby Pratt
Cover design: Brand Navigation
Interior design: Dina Sorn at Ahaa! Design

ISBN 978-0-7847-2283-1

15 14 13 12 11 10 09   9 8 7 6 5 4 3 2 1

Table of Contents

How to Use This Guide

This guide is designed for small group use with the companion book *Go!* It will help your group discuss the ideas from *Go!* and apply them in your lives. This happens best in groups that are growing together in real friendships, real faith, and real fun!

True to the Bible

The aim is not to study a book however. It is to study God's Word, using *Go!* as a launching pad. We have designed this guide, like all the Standard Publishing products you've come to trust, to be true to the Bible.

True to Life

We designed this guide also to be true to life—life in the real world of friends, spouses, disappointments, kids, jobs, bills, and other everyday circumstances. We want this guide to help your faith intersect with other aspects of your life so you will live the life that Jesus promised: life to the full!

A number of features make this guide distinctive:

✦ *It is designed for busy people.* You will not need to spend hours preparing for meetings, whether you are the leader or another member of the group. However, reading the companion book *Go!* is highly recommended to help you get the most out of this study.

✦ *It is designed for people at various maturity levels.* You do not need to be a Bible scholar to facilitate or participate in these studies. The companion book will provide the teaching for each session. Your job is to discuss the truths from God's Word and apply them to your life.

✦ *It is designed to develop community.* Your group—whether you are a Sunday school class, Bible study, or small group—will grow closer to one another as you share your stories, study the Word, and serve together. The optimal number of participants in a group is usually about three to ten, depending on a variety of circumstances. But larger groups can still be very effective. We suggest you subgroup if your group is larger than twelve. You may want to break into several groups of three to six during the Study and Apply sections, for instance, for deeper discussion and more authentic application.

✦ *It is designed to help you grow spiritually.* Real, lasting life change is the primary goal. The Holy Spirit will transform you as you allow him to work through God's Word and other group members to encourage, support, admonish, and pray for one another. Your group will employ Colossians 3:16: "Let the word of Christ dwell in you richly as you teach and admonish one another with all wisdom."

For the Leader

You are in a vital position to help people grow in their relationships with God. The best leadership comes out of the overflow of a godly leader's heart. The Leader Preparation section and other leader helps are included to feed *your* heart first—to equip and encourage you before you lead your group. God has called you to shepherd this small group of people that he has entrusted to your care. We want to provide whatever support and resources we can to help you carry out this vital ministry to which God has called you. We have several resources available to help meet your needs. Please visit http://www.standardpub.com/detail. aspx?ID=3194 to learn more about our small group help guides.

How Each Session Is Organized

Leader Preparation: Use this section to prepare your heart and mind for the meeting. To maximize opportunities for spiritual growth in your group, take time to read and reflect. Also use this time to pray for group members.

Bible Study Agenda: This study is designed to help participants *discover* truth from God's Word through group interaction rather than having the leader just *tell* them what it says. Participants will observe, contemplate, wrestle with, and take action on Scripture. Use the questions to facilitate lively interaction among group members. This will lead people to aha moments—when they *get it.* Ask follow-up questions to keep a good discussion moving. Keep the group on track with strong yet gentle encouragement and guidance.

+ *Connect:* Utilize the Connect activities to help group members share about what they know best—themselves—and to get them actively involved in the discussion. Since this study springboards from a game-show theme, your group should have a lot of fun by engaging one another through various Play It! and The $64,000 Question activities. Take advantage of the creative learning activities that best suit your group. The main question here is "What is your story?"

+ *Study:* These discussion questions are arranged to help members first observe and examine the Bible text, then understand and discern what the Scripture means and how they relate to it personally. The question here is "What is God saying to you in this passage?"

+ *Apply:* This is the most important meeting element. Make sure you move the group toward this part of the process. Here they will relate God's Word to their own everyday lives and decide what they will do with it. The question here is "How will I respond?"

+ *Game to Go:* Each session ends with a challenge for your group to take an action step that lives out the particular focus for the day. Some of these service opportunities that take the game show from the studio audience to the streets are very easy, and others will take some additional planning. The question here is "How are we going to reach others with God's truth in a practical way?"

Before the Next Meeting: Encourage group members to read the next chapter in *Go!* for the upcoming meeting. They may also look up Scripture passages if they like, but they do not need to do any other homework.

Leader's Between-Meeting Shepherding Ideas: A healthy, life-changing small group is more than just what happens during the meeting time. Set an example by staying in contact with participants between meetings though phone calls, visits, e-mail, and personal letters or cards. The best groups are like close families that care for one another 24/7.

The Price Is Right:
Go Sacrifice!

I have raised my hand to the LORD, God Most High, Creator of heaven and earth, and have taken an oath that I will accept nothing belonging to you, not even a thread or the thong of a sandal, so that you will never be able to say, "I made Abram rich."

—Genesis 14:22, 23

The goal of this session is to prepare ourselves to respond obediently to God's call. We will evaluate attachment to creature comforts and consider how easily we could give up the stuff we think we need to be happy. We will assess our willingness to respond to God's call, then look for ways he could be asking us to sacrifice.

Leader Preparation

Read Genesis 12–15:6 and Hebrews 11:8-16.

Read chapter 1 in the book *Go!* by Arron Chambers.

Pray with thanksgiving that God has called you to facilitate group discussion for this series. Whether or not you feel adequate or competent for this assignment, "The call of God is based not on what we've done but on the good works that we *will* do" (p. 19 in *Go!*). Expect that the blessing you receive will be greater than the sacrifice you make to prepare and lead your group.

For Creature Comforts—Bring to the session several of the following items: coffee mug; towel, shower cap, and bar of soap; comfortable shoes or slippers; afghan and pillow; chocolate candy bar.

For Play It!—Suggestions for a group version of The Price Is Right are on page 28 of *Go!* Review and make preparations to play the game.

Creature Comforts

The leader will display several items that represent creature comforts most of us take for granted. Make a list of five items you consider essential to your comfort. Which of these would you be most reluctant to give up, and why?

Brainstorm a list of various reasons people would choose to leave behind creature comforts for a cause. Here are a few to get you started:

✦ work out daily to lose weight or improve health

✦ get up in the middle of the night and stand out in the cold for an early-bird sale on the day after Thanksgiving

✦ stay up all night to care for a sick loved one

✦ sell everything and move to a foreign country to share Christ

✦ donate a kidney

✦ give up a career to care for a loved one

Discuss: What kinds of incentives do people need in order to make one of these sacrifices? In this session we will consider the call God gave to Abraham. We'll answer these questions: What motivated Abraham to obey and persevere? What incentives did he have? What kinds of sacrifices did he make, and why?

Play It!

To open the session, the leader will lead the group in a game of The Price Is Right.

Leader's Notes

This study focuses on the early chapters of Abraham's journey of faith. Both the disastrous plan to get a child through Hagar and the command to sacrifice Isaac were still in the future. Abraham's obedient responses to God in Genesis 12–15 give us plenty of examples to consider.

Melchizedek: We don't know precisely the identity of Melchizedek, although Hebrews 7:3 describes him as a type (specific symbol) for Jesus. The point is that Abraham was more than willing to let go of—sacrifice—the spoils of battle that technically belonged to him. Genesis 14:20 is the first mention of a tithe in the Bible.

● ● ● ● ● ● ● ● ● ● ● Study ● ● ● ● ● ● ● ● ● ● ●

The questions in this Study section trace the changes that took place in Abraham as he obeyed and sometimes doubted God's promise. The leader will assign each question to two group members who will read the Scriptures and prepare a summary to report to the rest of the group.

Read Genesis 12:1-5.

1. Compare God's command in verse 1 to Abraham's response in verses 4, 5. In your opinion how closely did Abraham follow God's command?

He took lot a nephew (raised like a son?)

Read Genesis 12:10–13:2.

2. What sacrifice was Abraham willing to make in Egypt? What could or

should have happened? What do you notice about the size of Abraham's entourage as he left Egypt?

Read Genesis 13:5-18.

3. What caused the dispute between Abraham and Lot? Who was willing to sacrifice? Why? How did God affirm this decision?

Read Genesis 14:11-24.

4. What sacrifice did Abraham make for Lot? What material goods did he bring back from this expedition? To whom did Abraham give a tithe (10 percent) of what he brought back? What attitude toward possessions and rewards did Abraham display in his conversation with the king of Sodom?

Read Genesis 15:1-6.

5. Describe the reward offered to Abraham in verse 1. Abraham wasn't counting on Lot to be his heir any longer. Who did he suggest instead? How did God respond? Compare the amount of detail God gave to Abraham in this encounter to the promise God made in Genesis 12:2, 3.

6. What do you learn about Abraham's expectations? What words describe how Abraham viewed himself? At what point do you think he began to recognize that God had something greater in store for him than being a rich landowner in Canaan?

• • • • • • • • • • • Apply • • • • • • • • • • •

7. Look back over your own faith walk with God. Have you observed gradual shifts in your understanding, or dramatic turning points? Did you sell out to God wholeheartedly at the very beginning, or have you been slow to submit and offer total obedience? What has most helped you to continue growing in your faith? In what specific ways does Abraham's example encourage you?

8. Discuss the difference between *making* a sacrifice and *being* a sacrifice. Abraham learned firsthand in Genesis 22, when God commanded him to sacrifice Isaac. These Scriptures might expand the discussion: Hebrews 13:15, 16; 1 Peter 2:5. Does learning to *make* a sacrifice prepare a person to embrace the totality of *being* a sacrifice? If so, how?

9. When Abraham first responded to God's call, he left without knowing where he was going (Hebrews 11:8). Can you identify with that kind of call from God—when you knew only that you needed to obey, but not where you would end up or what would come next? How did you feel? What was the outcome?

10. A certain percentage of us lean toward being control freaks. We want all the details before we launch anything new. Suggest some areas in which it can be difficult for you to let go. What practical advice would you offer someone who is reluctant to take the next step in a faith journey without more details from God?

11. What creature comforts could you let go of? What difference would it make if you made a small sacrifice—your daily specialty coffee, candy bar, or soda? What could you do with the money you saved?

Perhaps your group could pool some money and direct it toward a family in need. Maybe you could turn off your TV one night a week. Or give up some of your free time to visit an elderly person in a nursing home. You might make an effort to connect with a neighbor. Set a goal of making a sacrifice to honor God. It could be a first step in preparing you for God's next calling.

Search for a way to honor those in your community who have made sacrifices. For example:

✦ Take treats to a nearby fire station or police station. Thank those public servants for their willingness to sacrifice personal safety to protect and serve you and your neighbors.

✦ Find the family of a deployed soldier or an injured veteran. Inquire about ways your group can encourage and assist his or her family.

✦ Contact your local VFW or American Legion. They will help you with details so your group can write notes of encouragement and appreciation or prepare a care package to send to a service person.

Before the next meeting read chapter 2 in *Go!*

Win, Lose or Draw:
Go Lead!

"Watch me," he told them. "Follow my lead. . . . Do exactly as I do."

–Judges 7:17

The goal of this session is to challenge our reluctance to lead by focusing on God's mighty power to compensate and overcome our personal inadequacy and doubts.

Leader Preparation

Read Judges 6, 7.

Read chapter 2 in the book *Go!* by Arron Chambers.

Pray that through this session, group members will recognize that you depend on God to use you as their leader. Pray that God will open their eyes to ways he wants them to lead.

For Play It! (in Connect)—Prepare for a game of Win, Lose or Draw. Provide paper and a marker for every member. Keep the game moving—the point of this exercise is just to emphasize the idea that we all have fears and times when we feel inadequate. Sharing the full outcomes of the stories may have to be postponed until later. When individuals explain their drawings, have the group respond, "The Lord is with you, (say the person's name here), mighty warrior!" If your group is larger than eight, divide into two circles for sharing the drawings and explanations.

For Play It! (in Study)—Ahead of time, ask someone in the group to come prepared to give a brief review of the sequence of main events in Judges 6, 7. For this Win, Lose or Draw game, provide four permanent markers and four large sheets of paper (paper grocery bags work too). Write out the following Scripture references and image descriptions on four cards, one per card:

✦ Judges 6:21: food on rock/altar, with flames surrounding

✦ Judges 6:40: dry fleece on wet ground

✦ Judges 7:13, 14: rolling barley loaf and a sword

✦ Judges 7:16: torch, trumpet, and a jar

Play It!

The TV game show *Win, Lose or Draw* was based on the board game Pictionary. A fun way to begin this session is to have everyone in the group try their hand at drawing. The leader will provide paper and markers. Everyone in the group should quickly sketch a simple figure. The drawing should represent a situation in your life when you felt nearly paralyzed by fear. If possible have your drawing relate to something you felt God wanted you to do, but you were fearful and slow to obey. (There are no prizes for most artistic; stick figures are just fine.) After a couple of minutes of drawing, the leader should begin the sharing by showing his own drawing.

The $64,000 Question

Think about a time when you were assigned to a task or project. You felt as if you were the wrong person for the assignment. You felt sure you would fall flat on your face. Can you come up with two contrasting lines to describe your attitude or feelings before the project and after you completed it? Example: Before—"I felt sick to my stomach." After—"I felt hugely satisfied."

Leader's Notes

Midianites were descendants of Abraham and Keturah, the wife he married after the death of Sarah (Genesis 25:1-6). When Moses fled Egypt, he stayed with a priest of Midian and married his daughter (Exodus 2:15-21). Midian eventually united with Moab, turning against Israel (Numbers 22, 25).

Barley bread: The Midianite whose dream compared Israel's army to a loaf of barley bread shows how poor and hungry the Israelites were. Barley makes a bitter-tasting bread. It wouldn't be a big seller in the local bakery.

Read **Judges 6:6-16.**

1. What is ironic about the angel's greeting to Gideon? Suggest a title for Gideon that might have been more accurate.

2. Most times in the Bible when an angel arrived to deliver a message, the person was terrified. Gideon's initial reaction was almost argumentative: If God is with us, why are we so miserable and defeated? Notice the Lord's answer (vv. 14-16). Did God address Gideon's concerns? How was Gideon to be involved in the solution?

Read **Judges 6:17-27.**

3. Summarize the first test Gideon suggested. Did it remove Gideon's doubts?

4. What was the first assignment God gave to Gideon? How did Gideon respond? Read ahead through verse 32 and summarize the escalation of events begun by Gideon's response.

Skip over the fleece story (vv. 36-40). Many people remember only one part of the Gideon story—that he put out a fleece to make sure he understood what God wanted him to do. In fact, God does not command or encourage us to get our instructions from him through the fleece method. We have the Bible as our road map. We have prayer and the encouragement from other believers to guide us. The point of the fleece test was that Gideon twice more asked God to reassure him about what God had already promised to do: be with Gideon and win the battle for him.

Read Judges 7:1-8.

5. According to the Lord, what was the problem with the size of the army Gideon had assembled? What was the first method used for "troop reduction" in verse 3? Look ahead in verse 12 for a picture of the size of the Midianite force. Why was God setting up these impossible odds?

Read Judges 7:15-24.

6. Compare Gideon's attitude and actions in this section with earlier incidents. What differences do you notice?

7. What equipment did the soldiers carry? What is ironic about the soldiers crying out, "A sword for the LORD and for Gideon!"?

Play It!

The leader will ask the prepared group member to give a brief review of the sequence of main events in Judges 6, 7. Now it is Win, Lose or Draw time! Four volunteers can choose from the cards the leader has prepared and draw the indicated images on their papers. The audience will try to guess how each image fits into the story. Then the group can arrange the drawings in the correct sequence.

Follow the drawing activity with a discussion about God's willingness to show his power to Gideon. How did God prove himself to be trustworthy and powerful in the face of Gideon's fearful challenges? How does God show us that he will be with us today?

●●●●●●●●●● **Apply** ●●●●●●●●●●●

8. God's initial instructions to Gideon were: "Go in the strength you have" and "I will be with you" (Judges 6:14, 16). Those awesome promises still apply to us today. Read 2 Corinthians 12:9, 10. How would this testimony from Paul have been helpful to Gideon?

9. "Gideon's view of himself was so flawed, he couldn't make any sense of God's good opinion of him" (p. 36 in *Go!*). Which of these three descriptions from the life of Gideon do you most identify with?

○ scaredy-cat

○ worrier

○ mighty warrior

What do you need the most work on?

○ overcome flawed view of self

○ refocus on proper view of powerful and caring God

○ stop stalling and be willing to lead when God calls

Why did you answer as you did?

10. Read what the apostle Paul said in 1 Corinthians 11:1. Then compare Paul's words to what Gideon said in Judges 7:17. What advantage did Paul have?

11. What needs to ramp up in your life or be cut loose so you can say "Follow me!" as Gideon finally did?

Ramp up (check all that apply):

○ trust in God

○ involvement in sharing or serving

○ willingness to lead, even in a small way

○ memory of God's faithfulness in my life

○ other: _____

Cut loose (check all that apply):

○ longtime fears and doubts

○ complacency

○ feelings of not being worthy or good enough

○ other: _____

12. "Our God is a *more than* God!" (p. 36 in *Go!*). Use the following verses about God's power as reminders on your refrigerator or a mirror. Weave them into your prayers.

✦ Ephesians 3:20

✦ 1 John 4:4

✦ Jeremiah 32:17

Game to Go

Gideon conquered the Midianites to relieve the oppression of his people. In today's society some of those who struggle to survive are families led by single moms. How about adopting a single mom in your church or community who may feel very oppressed? A volunteer from your group should call such a mom and interview her about her greatest needs. Then set aside a Saturday for your group to overwhelm her with kindness. Here are some ideas:

✦ Tune up her car or tackle her list of around-the-house repairs.

✦ Send her to a salon for a haircut and pedicure while you take her kids to the park.

✦ Bring school supplies for her kids.

✦ Ask what housekeeping chore she hasn't be able to get to, and do it for her. Clean out the fridge or the garage, for example.

This mom's needs may not be met by one visit; aim to develop an ongoing friendship. You are mighty warriors—go accomplish this in the power of God!

Before the next meeting read Chapter 3 in *Go!*

Deal or No Deal:
Go Trust!

Do not take your servant for a wicked woman; I have been praying
here out of my great anguish and grief.

–1 Samuel 1:16

The goal of this session is to increase our trust quotient and to develop persistence and passion in our prayer lives.

Leader Preparation

Read 1 Samuel 1:1–2:11.

Read chapter 3 in the book *Go!* by Arron Chambers.

When you prepare a session like this one, focusing on prayer, you want to match your study preparation time with an equal amount of prayer preparation. Some of your group members, like Hannah in the Bible, carry the burden of deeply personal prayer concerns that may not have been answered as they hoped. Pray for your own tenderness toward those who might have bitterness toward God. You cannot change their hearts. Only God can lead each person into stronger trust.

For Play It!—To prepare to play Deal or No Deal, create a poster on which you write the following prizes: sundae at a local ice cream place, car wash, pot of flowers, specialty coffee (a la Starbucks), six people will pray for you for a week. Then cover the prize names by taping over the writing with five "suitcases" you have drawn on individual sheets of paper. Acquire the actual prizes (or their gift certificates) to give away. Also recruit or decide on six prayer warriors, and be sure to follow through with that part of the deal later.

Play It!

Play your own brief version of TV's *Deal or No Deal,* using the props the leader has prepared. You'll need a contestant from the group who is familiar with the TV game show, as well as a "producer" who will try to make the deal with the contestant to keep him from winning the fabulous prizes.

Afterwards, group members should assess the prizes and suggest a dollar value for each prize. Then consider these questions together: Isn't it funny how we value nearly everything more than we value prayer? What are some possible reasons that we don't esteem prayer as much as we should?

To finish this activity, the winner should write a prayer request on a card (or just write his name if the request is personal). The leader will deliver copies (or e-mail it) to the six prayer warriors.

The $64,000 Question

Discuss this question in your group: What's the longest amount of time you have ever prayed for something (meaning months or years, not six hours one night)?

Find the three people in your group who have prayed the longest for a single request. Ask them to share how God has answered those prayers. Ask them to comment on this question: What helps you remain confident in God when his answer to your prayer is delayed?

If any group members are still praying and waiting for God to act, others who are able can offer to meet with them individually, following your session, and pray with them about their ongoing requests.

Leader's Notes

The Lord's temple: the place of worship where Joshua had set up the tabernacle in the town of Shiloh (Joshua 18:1), located about halfway between Jerusalem and Samaria—not the temple to be built later by Solomon.

Barrenness: While infertility problems seem to be on the rise in our society, being unable to bear children in Bible times was disgraceful and considered a curse from God.

The name Samuel means "heard of God," or "asked God."

Read **1 Samuel 1:2-20.**

1. What reasons did Hannah have for being discouraged? Which do you think disturbed her more: the provocation she endured from wife number two or the failure and shame she felt at having no children? Why do you believe that?

2. How did Hannah respond to the ongoing disappointment in her life? Make a list of all Hannah's actions from verses 7-19. How many of them are negative? Which actions particularly demonstrate Hannah's trust in God?

3. What qualities or attributes of God did Hannah proclaim in her prayer? What various groups of people does this prayer say God deals with, and how does he respond to each group? What did Hannah ask for in this prayer?

4. Look for variety in the prayers Hannah prayed. Why is creativity and variety a good thing in prayer? What could make creativity and variety a not-so-good thing?

5. Read the following verses aloud. Members can each state which one speaks most directly into their own trust levels and prayer lives right now. How are Hannah's prayers connected to these verses?

✦ "Trust in him at all times, O people; pour out your hearts to him, for God is our refuge" (Psalm 62:8).

✦ "Do not be anxious about anything, but in everything, by prayer and petition, with thanksgiving, present your requests to God. And the peace of God, which transcends all understanding, will guard your hearts and your minds in Christ Jesus" (Philippians 4:6, 7).

6. People whose prayers are not answered in the way they'd like sometimes stop talking to God. How would you encourage someone in that situation? How could you use Hannah as an example—without coming across like, "Just keep begging, and God will give you what you want"?

7. Explore the difference between telling God what you want him to do (as if he's simply the genie in the sky) and asking him to show you how he would like to "make your dreams come true."

8. Read what David said in Psalm 27:13, 14. Compare his trust in God with Hannah's. What does biblical trust look like in your life? What is your next step? Check all that apply.

○ memorize Psalm 27:13, 14 to help me when my trust falters

○ take an action step of obedience

○ stay faithful right where I currently am

○ hang on until the storms pass

○ other: _____

9. "Hannah's passion for God helped her to keep trusting him. . . . Her passion carried her soul along as she waged a battle against bitterness" (p. 58 in *Go!*). Some Christians think they should ignore their own

passions (God-given passions) and dutifully "serve" God. Using another approach, accept the challenge to hone your passion. When was the last time you spent time doing something you truly love to do—fishing, reading a good book, having coffee with a friend you don't see often? Look at your schedule this week; pencil in a time to feed your passion. Remind yourself of how much you enjoy this activity. Thank God for the joy. Ask him to show you a way to use your passion to bring glory to him. Share your plan and passion with someone in your group. Next week that person will ask you if you took time to rekindle that passion.

10. "Hannah's prayer was a pledge of allegiance to God" (p. 55 in *Go!*). Write out your own prayer of allegiance, emphasizing a specific way you want to demonstrate your trust in God. Group members who are willing can read theirs aloud.

• • • • • • • • Game to Go • • • • • • • •

Hannah brought Samuel a new tunic every year when she visited Shiloh. Don't you wonder if she also brought him sandals, a new toothbrush, and a batch of his favorite cookies? As you travel or vacation in the near future, bring back all the small toiletry items provided by the hotel. Encourage others in your church to do the same. Then take your collection to a local safe shelter. Or create gift bags to donate to a homeless shelter in your area. Socks, toothbrushes, and pocket-size calendars are other valuable gifts to add for those who have no homes.

Before the next meeting read chapter 4 in *Go!*

Jeopardy!:
Go Risk!

I will go to the king, even though it is against the law. And if I perish, I perish.

–Esther 4:16

The goal of this session is to increase our confidence in God in order to increase our willingness to take risks for the kingdom.

Leader Preparation

Read the entire book of Esther (10 chapters).

Read chapter 4 in the book *Go!* by Arron Chambers.

Pray for God's plan to become evident in the lives of your group members. Pray that members will recognize God's hand at work and trust his wisdom and power.

For Play It!—For the "Esther version" of Jeopardy! refer to numbers 4–11 (below) and write on cards only the answers with the Scripture references. Make card numbers 1–3 and 12 for yourself.

1. Feast the Jews still celebrate, usually in March, to remember Esther. *What is Purim?*
2. Hissing and booing. *How do Jews react when Haman's name is mentioned during the reading of Esther on Purim?*
3. *Hamentaschen*, also known as Haman's hats. *What traditional cookies are made to celebrate Purim?* (They look like three-cornered hats.)
4. 180 days (Esther 1:4). *How long did the party go on before Xerxes ordered Vashti to join the party?*
5. Women would despise their husbands (Esther 1:17). *What is one reason Vashti had to be replaced?*

6. Hadassah, meaning "dove" (Esther 2:7). *What was Esther's Jewish name?*

7. Twelve months of beauty treatments, six with myrrh and six with perfumes and cosmetics (Esther 2:12). *How long did Esther prepare for her "interview" with the king?*

8. Ten thousand talents of silver (Esther 3:9). *How much money did Haman offer to Xerxes to get the king to agree to his plan to annihilate the Jews?*

9. Extend the gold scepter (Esther 4:11). *What action would the king take to show his willingness to spare someone's life?*

10. Zeresh (Haman's wife) and many friends (Esther 5:14). *Who gave Haman the suggestion to have the gallows built?*

11. Wear the king's robe and ride the king's horse (Esther 6:8, 10). *What is the reward Haman wanted that Mordecai received?*

12. A fifth-century-BC holocaust. *What is the "ultimate solution" Haman had planned for the Jews?*

For Advertising Agency—Write these key words on a board or poster: orphan, contest, king, villain, hero, heroine, thrill, and rescue. Also provide pens and paper.

•••••••••• Connect ••••••••••

Play It!

Play an "Esther version" of Jeopardy! The leader will distribute cards to group members, who will look up the verses and write the question that matches the answer. The leader will introduce the game himself with three questions. Then members will take turns reading their answers and giving others the opportunity to come up with the correct questions. The leader will wrap up the game with a final question.

Advertising Agency

Esther is a unique book in the Bible. It reads almost like a soap opera or a melodrama. In order to put ourselves into the middle of the story, we'll pretend to be writers. Each person should work with two or three other writers to compose the advertisement for a made-for-TV movie about Esther. The leader will provide some helpful key words to include in the ads. Teams can review the sample ad here and take several minutes to compose their own ads. Then share. Sample:

> Esther is a story quite unlike any other Bible story. It's a soap opera and melodrama rolled into one. We meet a beautiful orphan who wins a beauty contest and becomes queen. There's an evil villain, a careless king, and a faithful caretaker. There's a plot for genocide and some remarkable coincidences. In the end the queen overcomes her fears, tackles corruption in her government, and saves her people from annihilation.

The $64,000 Question

Risk management is big business. Financial companies diversify their assets in order to avoid losses. Public buildings install sprinkler systems to avoid the risk of fire damage or loss of life. Hospitals maintain precautions to minimize risks for patients and workers. Local governments prepare emergency contingency plans to minimize danger in times of natural disaster.

What should be the Christian's approach to risk management in personal life? Should we have a different view of risk taking because of our belief that God is in control?

What is the biggest risk you've ever taken? How did it turn out?

● ● ● ● ● ● ● ● ● ● ● ● **Study** ● ● ● ● ● ● ● ● ● ● ●

Leader's Notes

God's name is not mentioned in Esther's story, but his presence is unmistakable.

Schedule a movie night for your group to view *One Night with the King*. If your group is made up of families with young kids, the VeggieTales movie *Esther, the Girl Who Became Queen* would make it a fun family night.

The irrevocable laws of the Medes and the Persians created a stumbling block for Xerxes. When Esther revealed that he had signed into law a plan that would kill her people, Xerxes could not simply repeal the law. Xerxes could add new laws but could not revoke the original one (also see Daniel 6:8). The king sort of washed his hands of the problem and turned it over to Esther and Mordecai to come up with a solution.

Read > Esther 3:1-6 and 4:1-8.

1. "We weren't designed by God to play it safe" (p. 63 in *Go!*). What risks did Mordecai take? In what ways did he go above and beyond the call of duty? How do you suppose his example influenced Esther's decision to be a risk taker?

2. Esther's physical beauty blossomed during her year of beauty treatments. Her winsome personality made her a favorite in the harem. Read 1 Peter 3:3, 4. How did Esther exemplify the qualities mentioned? In your opinion, which counted the most in her plan to go to the king: her external beauty or her inner beauty? Explain.

Read > Esther 5:1-8.

3. What are some possible reasons that Esther chose not to immediately tell the king her reason for risking her life to speak with him? Do you think she had the dinner-with-king-and-Haman plan before she went in, or did she think it up on the spot? Why do you say that?

Read ▸ Esther 8:1-11.

4. How did Esther and Mordecai deal with the plan Haman had set in place for the destruction of the Jews?

Read ▸ Esther 10:3.

5. What reputation and power did Mordecai have at the end of the book? Review his actions and choices throughout the circumstances. How did his integrity and perseverance pay off?

• • • • • • • • • • • Apply • • • • • • • • • • •

6. You have come to royal position for such a time as this" (4:14). It was very clear to Mordecai that Esther's ascension to royalty was no accident. Have you ever been in a situation where it seemed God had orchestrated the circumstances? Does that make it easier or more challenging to follow through and take the risk? Why?

7. "If you remain silent . . ." (4:14). How would you rate yourself in the category of speaking up? In what way could you stretch your ability to be

bold? Do you need to improve your ability to listen and reflect before blurting out your first reaction? How do you think Esther's preparation and "staging" played into the outcome?

8. Volunteers can read the following verses aloud. All group members should note character traits or actions of a risk taker:

✦ 2 Corinthians 3:12

✦ 2 Corinthians 4:1

✦ 2 Corinthians 4:18

✦ Colossians 4:5

✦ Hebrews 11:16, 26

Which of these were evident in the life of Esther? in the life of Mordecai?

Session 3 included the challenge to take time to rekindle your passion. Group members who discussed this last time should ask each other whether they were able to follow through with their assignments.

Game to Go

Because cookies are part of the modern-day celebration of the story of Esther, schedule a secret cookie-drop-off night. Have everyone bring a batch of cookie dough and a cookie sheet. Be prepared with sturdy disposable plates and plastic bags (or wrap) for covering the cookies. While some members are getting the cookies ready to bake, others should be planning the routes for the secret drop-offs. Others can write cards of thanks or encouragement.

As the cookies cool, arrange a dozen on each plate and cover them. Attach cards saying: "From friends at _____ Church who appreciate you" or simply "In the name of Jesus." Drop off plates of freshly baked cookies at the homes of the elderly, church leaders, or youth coaches. But it's secret. Place the plates on the porch, ring the doorbell . . . and run! As you end the night eating the leftovers, pray for those families to whom you delivered cookies. And pray that your group will be willing to take *real* risks for God's kingdom and glory.

Before the next meeting read chapter 5 in *Go!*

I've Got a Secret:
Go Tell!

The women hurried away from the tomb, afraid yet filled with joy,
and ran to tell his disciples.

—Matthew 28:8

The goal of this session is to become motivated to overcome the fear of sharing our faith, to spur us to refine our own faith messages, and to increase our reliance on God to open doors for us.

Leader Preparation

Read Matthew 28:1-15; Mark 16:1-8; Luke 24:1-12; and John 20:19-23.

Read chapter 5 in the book *Go!* by Arron Chambers.

Pray that you will look at the resurrection with fresh eyes, not as a repeat of a familiar story. Pray that the renewed impact of this pivotal historical moment on your faith will strengthen your resolve to share the significance with those around you who don't know the secret.

For Play It!— See page 89 in *Go!* You'll find a plan for having your group participate in the I've Got a Secret game to get your session started. Provide pens and paper.

For Apply—There won't be time to do everything in this section. Review and select two or three options that will work best for your group. (Paper and pens are needed for number 7.) Try to include number 8.

Connect

Play It!

Open this session by playing a game of I've Got a Secret, as directed by the leader.

The $64,000 Question

Who told you the secret? Tell about the person who first shared Jesus with you, helping you get started on your faith journey.

Study

Read ▸ **Mark 16:1-4.**

1. Why were the women going to the tomb? What preparation had they made? What fears do you think they had as they approached the tomb? What problem were they discussing? How was their trip to the tomb a faith journey?

Read ▸ **Matthew 28:1-10.**

2. What specific information did the angel give the women? What specific commands did the angel give?

3. "Their prayers had been answered, their grief had been executed" (p. 88 in *Go!*). Describe the women's return into Jerusalem. According to verse 8, what different emotions did they have? What was their mission?

Read **Luke 24:1-12.**

4. How did the apostles respond to the women's great news? Why do you think the men were skeptical? Why did they doubt the women? Why do you suppose God's plan was for the women to receive the news and deliver it to the apostles rather than the other way around? (Don't let this turn into a battle of the sexes!)

Read **Matthew 28:11-15.**

5. What did the Jewish religious leaders want to keep secret? How did they try to accomplish that?

Read **John 20:19-23.**

6. What did the disciples want to keep secret? Why? How did Jesus help them?

Leader's Notes

It's ironic that God chose women to be the first to go tell about Jesus' resurrection. In the first century, women were not permitted to testify in a court of law. They were considered unreliable and unstable as witnesses. They had very few rights; their lives were under the control of their fathers or their husbands. Jesus' treatment of women began to change those restrictions and attitudes.

7. Evangelism training used to consist of a class that involved memorizing Bible verses, specific techniques, and steps to take in "soul winning." Today's culture seems more open to the sharing of personal stories and discussions of spirituality. Divide into groups of two or three. Each group should take about ten minutes to summarize God's story and plan into ten sentences or less. Share your results with each other.

8. Individuals who are not yet believers may be more open to hearing the story of your own life as a first step before you get an opportunity to talk about Jesus. Write your own story in three sentences:

✦ What your life was like before you met Jesus—

✦ How you met Jesus—

✦ What your life is like since he has been in charge—

Take a few minutes to practice telling your three-sentence stories.

9. Read the Bible verses listed below. What if you could use only one verse to tell someone about Jesus? Which one would you choose? Why? Can you think of any other verses that might be appropriate?

○ "For God so loved the world that he gave his one and only Son, that whoever believes in him shall not perish but have eternal life" (John 3:16).

○ "You killed the author of life, but God raised him from the dead. We are witnesses of this" (Acts 3:15).

○ "Christ died for our sins according to the Scriptures, . . . was buried, . . . was raised on the third day according to the Scriptures" (1 Corinthians 15:3, 4).

○ "This is how God showed his love among us: He sent his one and only Son into the world that we might live through him" (1 John 4:9).

○ "This is the testimony: God has given us eternal life, and this life is in his Son" (1 John 5:11).

○ Other:

Our society sometimes limits the Christian's ability to tell the secret. Many professions have rules about what you can do and say in your workplace concerning your faith. A counselor who works in a clinic for addicts told that she felt frustrated because she couldn't openly share her faith with her clients. As she drove home from a session, she was praying for a solution to the limitations. A song came on the radio that included Romans 2:4: God's kindness leads us to repentance. The counselor felt that she'd received an answer to her prayers. She could show kindness to her clients in unexpected ways. That could lead them to ask questions or to discover God's love. She committed herself to plant seeds of kindness and ask God to grow a harvest.

10. As a group, suggest ways to honor God and live your faith in places where talking about faith is not appropriate.

11. "As we tell the good news, it's OK to share the secret that we had to face our fears to do so" (p. 85 in *Go!*). The fear factor. Many Christians remain

silent, afraid they will fail if they open their mouths and share their faith. What are some possible ways to reduce the fear factor?

Talk to God about the fears that create the most anxiety for you. Tell God you will share your story and his story in spite of your fear. Select two or three people in your life who need to know Jesus. Commit to praying for them regularly. Ask God to use you even though you may feel inadequate. Close your group with prayer focused on the individuals you have committed to pray for and speak to.

Game to Go

How many Bibles are lying around your house? How many do you really need? According to the Christian Resource Institute, "the average American Christian owns nine Bibles and is actively in the market for more." Many churches in foreign countries can use English Bibles. Your group could search their bookshelves and closets for extra Bibles they would be willing to donate to an organization like CRI (www.cribooks.homestead.com/bareyourbookshelf.html). Your group may decide to sponsor a Bible drive for your entire church. Those who do not have an extra Bible to give away could donate toward shipping costs.

Before the next meeting read chapter 6 in *Go!*

What's My Line?:
Go Work!

You will receive power when the Holy Spirit comes on you;

and you will be my witnesses.

—Acts 1:8

The goal of this session is to enlarge our perspective of ways in which we can work as God's ambassadors in our workplaces. We will come away with confidence that God will provide the power and strength. Each member will have the opportunity to define his own role in the "ministry of reconciliation."

Leader Preparation

Read Acts 1:1-11.

Read chapter 6 in the book *Go!* by Arron Chambers.

Pray for a new attitude about your own career. If you have that all-important career of being a stay-at-home mom, ask God to remind you that this is significant kingdom work. If you dislike your job, ask God to show you one way you can make a difference for the kingdom in your workplace. If you love your job and coworkers, thank God for that blessing. Ask him to open your eyes to small ways through which you can point coworkers toward Jesus.

For Play It!—You will recruit a few volunteers to play the part of the guests for several rounds of What's My Line? The guests should review the following list of Bible occupations and each select one they feel comfortable answering questions about: fisherman, tax collector, carpenter, queen, tentmaker, shepherd, prophet, treasurer, cupbearer, priest, soldier, musician, pharaoh, servant, rabbi, farmer.

You may opt to play Hangman instead, using the same list of Bible occupations. In this case, supply a large pad of paper (or white board) and marker.

Play It!

Play What's My Line? with a theme of Bible occupations. Divide your group into two or three teams. The leader will recruit volunteers to be the guests. Each team can ask five questions with yes/no answers to attempt to discover the guests' occupations. Play several rounds.

Follow with a brief discussion of this question: In how many of these jobs can we see a way that this worker could have been used by God to perform a specific task for God's kingdom?

The $64,000 Question

What was your very first job? How much did you get paid? How did your first job influence your choice of a career?

Read **Acts 1:1-3.**

1. Based on these verses, below is a to-do list for Jesus' forty days on earth after his resurrection. What else do you suppose Jesus would have included as essential? What tasks do you think were the most important?

○ teaching

○ giving instructions through the Holy Spirit

○ appearing to people

○ giving many convincing proofs

○ speaking about the kingdom of God

○ other: _____

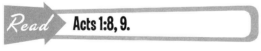
Read ▶ **Acts 1:4, 5.**

2. During a meal with the apostles, Jesus gave a two-part command. What was the negative and what was the positive?

3. Then Jesus contrasted the previous era with the new era. What event was in the past, and what new activity of God was soon to happen? What do you imagine was going on in the minds of the apostles concerning this prediction?

Read ▶ **Acts 1:6, 7.**

4. Based on the question the apostles asked, how do you think they were interpreting the instructions Jesus had just given them?

5. How did Jesus deal with their question?

Read ▶ **Acts 1:8, 9.**

6. What was Jesus' final promise? What was his final instruction?

7. How are the promise and the instruction related?

8. Compare the details of this scene with Matthew 28:16-20. Does it comfort you to know that the apostles worshiped, but some doubted? How so?

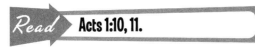

Read **Acts 1:10, 11.**

9. In your opinion, why were the angels necessary?

10. Why do you suppose the angels addressed the apostles as "men of Galilee" instead of "apostles chosen by Christ and ready to accomplish his mission"?

11. In summary, note the promises contained in Acts 1:4-11. How would you have reacted to that information, had you been present?

Leader's Notes

Luke is the only writer to include the detail that Jesus' time on earth after the resurrection was forty days in length.

Christians don't all agree on issues surrounding baptism. But we do agree that it is our faith in Jesus' death and resurrection that frees us from sin. And it is the Holy Spirit's presence in our individual lives that empowers, guides, and produces godly character within us. The coming of the Holy Spirit on the Day of Pentecost as recorded in Acts 2 did several things:

+ fulfilled prophecy and promise
+ signaled a new era in God's plan for humankind
+ announced the birthday of the church

All believers receive the Holy Spirit, but the three miraculous signs of that day—the sound of the mighty rushing wind, the flames of fire over the heads of the apostles, and their supernatural ability to speak in tongues—do not accompany every conversion experience.

After his audience believed his sermon and accepted their guilt, Peter told them to repent and be baptized for forgiveness of sins and the gift of the Holy Spirit. In Acts 19:1-7 Paul also connected baptism with the presence of the Holy Spirit.

If your group has questions concerning how the Holy Spirit and baptism are related, schedule a session to study and discuss those specific topics. Some resources for further study include:

✦ *Don't Divorce the Holy Spirit* by Knofel Staton
✦ *Names of the Holy Spirit* by Elmer Towns
✦ *Names of the Holy Spirit* by Ray Pritchard

●●●●●●●●●● Apply ●●●●●●●●●●●

Read **2 Corinthians 12:9, 10.**

12. How do we access the power of the Spirit in our lives? How should we put that power to use? Through God's power, what weaknesses in your own life and witness have you had some successes in overcoming?

Read **2 Corinthians 3:5, 6.**

13. What encouragement do these verses give us about overcoming our in-competence?

14. How does this promise apply to you? Should you leave it up to the Spirit or plan out what to say? Explain.

15. "God always gives us all the power we need for any job he calls us to do" (p. 95 in *Go!*). What roles or "job descriptions" are given to believers in this text? Are these for all believers or only a special group? Is the "ministry of reconciliation" broader than a basic message to repent and accept Jesus? How would you define your role in the ministry of reconciliation?

16. Recall times when you have felt urgent about sharing your faith. What brought about that sense of urgency? What enabled you to be bolder? What limits your willingness to be a witness?

• • • • • • • • Game to Go • • • • • • • •

Commit to pray for your workplace for a week, perhaps on your way to work. Ask God to help you see your office or customers through his eyes. Ask him to show you what specific plans he has for you in this job.

Look for a practical way you can bless your workplace. Check out these suggestions:

✦ Invite several coworkers to eat lunch with you. You don't need an evangelistic agenda. Simply determine to get better acquainted and improve workplace morale.

✦ Think about how you can brighten up your workplace. If your office has a break room or kitchen, take time before or after work to secretly clean up the area. Clean out the refrigerator. Bring in an encouraging poster. Display a bulletin board of fun cartoons.

✦ If you have a hard-to-get-along-with coworker, commit to pray for that person for a month. Ask God to give you the power to show kindness to that individual.

✦ If you are a stay-at-home mom, ask God to show you his presence as you nurture your children. Look for opportunities to point out how God helps your family throughout the day. Ask God to open doors in your neighborhood to share his love.

Before the next meeting read chapter 7 in *Go!*

Don't Forget the Lyrics!:
Go Obey!

The apostles left the Sanhedrin, rejoicing because they had been
counted worthy of suffering disgrace for the Name.

–Acts 5:41

The goal of this session is to evaluate our own willingness to "sing the song" at any
cost. We will each choose a way to be more obedient to God.

Leader Preparation

Read Acts 5:14-42. Note the way the Scripture is divided into scenes in the Study section below.

Read chapter 7 in the book *Go!* by Arron Chambers.

Pray for your own boldness in delivering the gospel message. Ask God to increase your reliance on his power and to decrease your fear of negative responses.

For Play It!—Ahead of time, select two contemporary Christian songs that emphasize grace or salvation through Jesus. Bring a CD player and CDs or an iPod and iPod dock in order to play these for your group.

For Missing Lyrics—Ahead of time, make two identical sets of cards, printing the lyrics from a well-known song, one line per card. Purposely remove one card from each set. Then mix up the order of the cards. As group members play the game, stop the game when they figure out that part of the song is missing.

For Study—There probably won't be time to do both number 1 and number 2. Review these and choose the one that's best for your group.

Play It!

The leader will play the songs he has chosen. Group members should listen for an emphasis on grace or salvation and jot down phrases that have personal significance. How could you use these lyrics to prepare yourself to share your faith with someone?

The $64,000 Question

Group members should each choose one of these questions to answer:

✦ As you were growing up, what was the worst punishment you ever received for disobeying?

✦ What is the worst persecution or ridicule you've ever had to endure because you are a Christian?

✦ If you are a musician, tell about a time when you forgot your music, forgot the words, or made a noticeable mistake during a performance. Did that experience "scar" you, or did you get over it?

Missing Lyrics

Divide the group into two teams. Teams will each use a set of the cards the leader has prepared and compete to see who can put the lyrics in order the fastest. After the game, discuss: In chapter 7 in *Go!* the lyrics illustrate the idea of Christians sharing their faith, or telling the gospel story. What happens when believers forget part of the story?

Read ▶ **Acts 5:14-42.**

1. Each group member (or small team) can be assigned one of the following scenes from Acts 5. Then brainstorm songs that would be played on the soundtrack if this story were made into a movie.

Scene 1 (vv. 14-16)—Growing popularity, healings:

Scene 2 (vv. 17, 18)—Jealousy brings arrests:

Scene 3 (vv. 19-21a)—An angel sends them back to speak:

Scene 4 (vv. 21b-24)—No prisoners to punish:

Scene 5 (vv. 25-28)—Rearrested and reprimanded:

Scene 6 (vv. 29-33)—Peter's message:

Scene 7 (vv. 34-39)—Gamaliel's advice:

Scene 8 (v. 40)—The punishment:

Scene 9 (v. 41)—Praise for the privilege:

Scene 10 (v. 42)—Punishment and threats can't stop the message:

2. Put Peter's message to music. Divide into teams of three or four. Choose a familiar song. Replace the lyrics with Peter's message in Acts 5:29-33.

3. The Jewish leaders intended that the severe beating the apostles received would stop their preaching, or at least slow them down. They were making an example out of these "troublemakers." According to verse 42, did their plan work? Why do you suppose the believers were not intimidated?

Leader's Notes

According to Acts 23:8, the Sadducees denied the existence of angels. God could have simply opened the prison door, or caused an earthquake as in Acts 16. Instead, he chose to use angels. Maybe God likes the ironic touch.

Flogging: Jesus endured flogging before the crucifixion. The Jews limited the torture to thirty-nine lashes. They thought forty would be enough to kill a person (also see Deuteronomy 25:1-3). The whip had multiple lashes, leather strips tied with bits of bone or metal, essentially ripping open the victim's back. The person who performed the whipping was called the lictor. The phrase *took a licking* comes from that word. Paul records that he was flogged by the Jews five times (2 Corinthians 11:24).

●●●●●●●●● Apply ●●●●●●●●●

4. The apostles did not let threats and prison change their plans. They knew that they were to continue to spread the message because an angel specifically commanded them to return to the temple and continue preaching. Most of us today do not have the benefit of an angelic messenger. We tend to interpret opposition as a sign from God that the door is closed. What could change our attitude toward opposition? In what ways should our plans change when the audience responds negatively to our message?

5. Consider Peter's later writings about suffering. From each of the following verses, summarize Peter's attitude toward enduring persecution as a believer. Circle the verse that stands out as most significant to you.

✦ 1 Peter 2:21

✦ 1 Peter 3:14

✦ 1 Peter 4:16

✦ 1 Peter 4:19

How should Peter's encouragement change our attitudes toward persecution?

The angel commanded the apostles to "tell the people the full message" (Acts 5:20). Sometimes in today's world, the message is diluted or distorted by the lack of obedience in the life of the messenger. Actions really do speak louder than words.

6. Review the section "Obedience" in chapter 7 of *Go!* (p. 108). How is a lifestyle of obedience crucial to telling "the full message"? Conversely, how does a disobedient lifestyle detract from sharing the gospel? Consider one particular way you could enhance your ability to share your faith by improving your obedience to God.

7. What song could be the theme of your life, and why?

In session 5 we developed three-sentence testimonies. Now would be a great time for group members to review their stories with the group.

Game to Go

Women of the Harvest is a support organization that encourages and serves women involved in foreign mission fields. They encourage through an online newsletter and sponsor several retreats every year. Visit www.womenoftheharvest.com to see when and where they will hold their next retreat. Your group can collect and send items that will be given away during the retreat. These are treats like chocolate and peanut butter, lotions and cosmetics. These items seem common to us, but are hard for women in distant places to get. You can also commit to pray for the organization's upcoming events.

Visit the Web site of Voice of the Martyrs, www.persecution.com, an organization aiding Christians who are persecuted for their faith. Choose several situations that your group could pray for. What opportunities could your group get involved with?

Before the next meeting read chapter 8 in *Go!*

The Moment of Truth:
Go Serve!

Brother Saul, the Lord—Jesus, who appeared to you on the road as you
were coming here—has sent me so you may see again.

—Acts 9:17

The goal of this session is to challenge ourselves to serve whenever and wherever
God calls, in big and small ways, in public and private ways, in ways that will pull
us out of our comfort zones.

Leader Preparation

Read Acts 9:1-18 and 22:12-16.

Read chapter 8 in the book *Go!* by Arron Chambers.

Pray for willing hearts for yourself and your group.

For Play It!— Before your session, jot down the actions listed below, each on a separate slip of
paper. Place the papers in a basket: changing a tire, washing windows, feeding someone who is
hungry, giving someone a ride, delivering groceries, raking the yard, painting someone's house,
shoveling snow.

For Two Truths and a Lie—Prepare a prize for the person voted for in this game. The prize could
be an Almond Joy bar to signify joy in serving, or a roll of Life Savers.

●●●●●●●●●●● ● Connect ● ●●●●●●●●●●●

Play It!

Play a game of charades, in which the theme is various acts of service. Divide the group into two teams. Team members draw slips of paper out of a basket the leader has prepared. Then individuals silently act out the act of service and have the others on their team try to guess the activity. Keep score.

Two Truths and a Lie

Each person should think of three ways he or she has been involved in helping someone. Two of the statements should be true, and one should be a lie. Take turns having people announce their three statements to the group. The group guesses which are true and which is the lie. Then vote to determine the person with the most unusual true example of serving.

●●●●●●●●●● ●● Study ● ●●●●●●●●●●●

God assigned Ananias to a significant service project. The only problem with the project was the recipient. He was a murderer, and some of Ananias's friends were on his hit list. What would it take to change Ananias's heart to be ready to serve?

Read ▶ Acts 9:10-16.

1. When God spoke to Ananias in a vision, Ananias already seemed well informed about Saul (who would later be called Paul). What did Ananias know, and what reasons did he have for wishing God had given the vision to someone else? Who else had received a vision? How did the two visions intersect?

2. What details did God reveal that would help Ananias gain confidence in the mission he was called to?

3. How did God answer Ananias's objections? Or did he?

Read ▶ **Acts 9:8, 9.**

4. How do you imagine Saul's physical condition when Ananias arrived to see him? What do you suppose his spiritual condition was?

Read ▶ **Acts 9:17, 18.**

5. Ananias entered the house of a man named Judas, laid hands on Saul, and called him "brother." What does this indicate to you about Ananias's heart and his willingness to obey God's direction?

Read ▶ **Acts 22:12-16.**

6. In this flashback, Paul is recalling his conversion. How did Paul describe Ananias in verses 12, 13?

7. Compare Ananias's message in verses 14-16 with Acts 9:13-19. What added details do you learn? At what point in these accounts do you think Ananias became unafraid of Saul? Or did he?

8. What sort of impact do you think Ananias had on Saul? How do you think Saul impacted Ananias?

Leader's Notes

There is still a Straight Street in Damascus, Syria.

Acts 9:13 is the first mention of Christians as "holy ones," later translated as "saints."

The NIV Application Commentary notes that "God's arrangements are confirmed by a double vision. Visions occur often in Acts when God intervenes to direct the church into something new" (p. 299, Zondervan, 1998).

•••••••••• Apply •••••••••••

9. "God has a plan for your life—and it's not to sit around and collect dust until you assume room temperature" (p. 121 in *Go!*). How do you respond to assignments from God? Check all that apply.

O quick to obey

O need more details; try to negotiate

O stall, hoping God will ask someone else

O try to get a friend to do it with me

O say, "No way!" and wait for lightning to strike

10. Tell about a time when you were reluctant to get involved in serving someone but God used you and blessed you as you served. How did it turn out? What did you learn about yourself?

11. Some Christians think they must say yes to every request for help that comes their way. How do you decide when to say yes and when to say no? Some Christians think they should volunteer only in an area where they are gifted. Do you agree or disagree? Why?

12. This account is the only time that Ananias is mentioned. He is the minor character; Saul is the main character (although Ananias does have more lines than Judas, who owned the house). How difficult is it for you to accept a behind-the-scenes role? What can you learn from Ananias about the importance of roles that might seem small to you?

13. On the other hand, some of us are more than content to remain behind the scenes. We live in dread that God will call us to a situation that is bigger than we want to handle. What can you do to prepare for God's call, big or small?

Game to Go

Look for ways to serve people, ways that are out of your comfort zone. Here are some suggestions:

✦ Some people can't stand to enter nursing homes. They imagine bad-smelling places where elderly people sit in their wheelchairs in the hall and cry out to you or reach for your hand. Connect with a facility where your group can deliver some small gifts to the residents—a flower, a small stuffed animal, a postcard-size picture. Offer to read the Bible or write a note for a person who doesn't see well.

✦ Some people are fearful and suspicious of homeless people. Ask your local police department about finding a likely location where homeless people congregate. Prepare sack lunches and distribute them. Make a point to ask the people their names, and offer to pray for them.

✦ Plan a parents' night out for families in your community who have children with disabilities. You'll need the participation of your entire group. You may also want to secure some staff help from the church, especially someone who has experience in working with children with special needs. Reserve several rooms at your church building. Invite the families to leave all their children. Get a complete list of instructions from parents, as well as any dietary restrictions. Order pizza for the majority. Plan games for both small and large groups. Assign specific pairs to care for individual children. As the evening progresses, move toward story time or show a video. Bring some sleeping bags or blankets for younger children to rest on. You will bring a huge blessing to parents who will enjoy having a rare evening alone, knowing their children are well cared for.

Bonus Project
Have a Backstage Bash!

One effective way for taking the game show out of the audience and into the streets is by uniting in teamwork and service to throw a Backstage Bash! Your group can prepare a celebration, complete with a game-show host. Connect with families in your community by hosting an incredible outreach event that includes . . .

+ Great food

+ Fun music

+ Family-friendly crafts

+ Games and activities

+ Family service projects

You can even order a kit for this outreach at:

http://vbs09.vacationbibleschool.com/

Here's what you'll get:

◆ A 24-page leader's guide filled with practical tips and creative options for games, food, crafts, family service projects, and more!

◆ A CD-ROM packed with color graphics, eps images, and modifiable pdfs to publicize and decorate your Backstage Bash event. Also contains printable volunteer helps and a custom photo border to send home as a family souvenir!

◆ A colorful vinyl tablecloth covered with games that families and friends can play over and over again (also sold separately).

What a perfect way to celebrate the end of this study!